SOMEPLACE Strange ™

written by
Ann Nocenti

illustrated by
John Bolton

edited by
JO DUFFY
MARK CHIARELLO

lettered by
TOM ORZECHOWSKI

logo design by
GRAHAM MARKS

book design by
ROBBIN BROSTERMAN

editor in chief
ARCHIE GOODWIN

published by Epic Comics, Inc.
a New World Company
387 Park Avenue South
New York, NY 10016
ISBN #0-87135-439-X

Psssst!
Yeah, you. Climb out your window . . .
Out on this limb
What's that sound, is it your own heart?
What's wrong, scared? Dizzy? Good!
You sleepyhead, lumpensludge, deadweight, clinging vine
Shake off those body rags and start sparking!
Get scared, get dizzy, get up, get wild!
Time for razzmatazz and soft shoe shuffle
Come to where life is as light as a star's wink,
As heavy as the belly of a black hole.
Imagine yourself out past the night
Swirling in clouds of shuddering particle chaos,
The eternal junkyard of the gods
Watching stars struggle to resist each other's pull . . .
Give in, take up orbit—and collide!
Subatomics smash, shatter and scream
Gasses mix and breathe each other
A private molten birth—the birth of a new star!
But if you stay home, if you don't go,
You'll only see the rosy aftermath
In the twinkle of a far away star
That may no longer exist
That has long since collapsed
A million years late
The power that creates a star, gravity, can also
Crush you to your chair
So get up, come touch the tips of alice's fingers
Come, let's go someplace strange . . .
—ANN NOCENTI

4

6

7

9

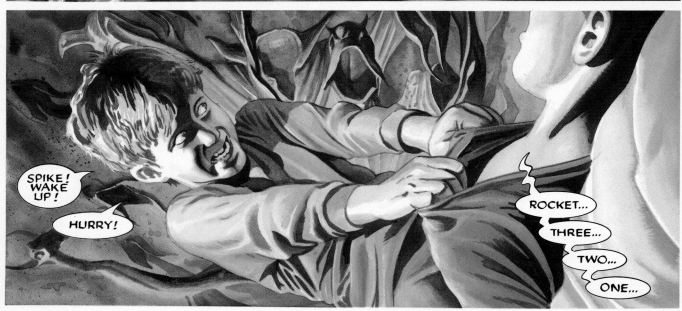

10

14

YEAH. YOUR BOGEY'S DOWN HERE. ALWAYS THRASHIN' AN' BANGIN'-- NEVER LETS ME SLEEP.

HEY-- YOU'RE JUST A NORMAL GIRL. YOU LIVE HERE? DON'T YOUR PARENTS WORRY--?

I KILLED THEM.

OH.

UH... YOU EVER BEEN DOWN HERE, uh, MISS...

JOY. MY NAME'S JOY. AN' YOUR NAMES ARE DIRTBAG AN' JERKFACE, RIGHT?

YEAH.

YEAH, RIGHT.

JUST A STUPID, DULL, ORDINARY, OLD BASEMENT.

HEY, GUYS...

SLAM

AAAAAAAAAAA EEEEEEEEEE YELP?!

PLIP

15

19

WATCH OUT! DIVE BOMBERS!

SPUTCH-SQWUSH!

I THINK THEY'RE EATING CAKE.

JOY! YOU GOTTA *SHAKE* THIS *BAD MOOD* YOU'RE IN, OR THIS WORLD'S GONNA KEEP *ATTACKING* US!

SHUT UP! I'M *ALWAYS* IN A BAD MOOD!

I'M STUCK HERE, AN' I CAN'T SHAKE IT, AN' IT'S ALL THIS JERK'S FAULT!

STUPID WORLD! I HATE IT! I HATE YOU BOYS!

HATE HATE HATE!

STOP SHOUTING!

YOUR WORDS ARE *PUSHING* HIM!

NO! COME BACK!

SO WHAT? GOOD RIDDANCE!

THAT'S MY ONLY *BROTHER* YOU BLEW AWAY!

SHUT UP. IT WAS *FUN.*

24

25

26

SQUIWOOSH!

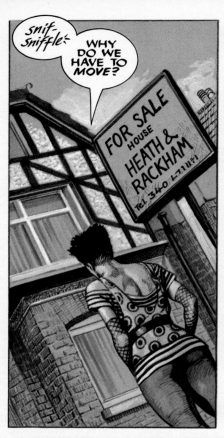

34

36

37

38

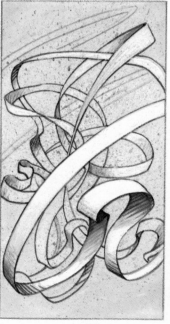

WOULD ANYONE ELSE CARE FOR A SHOT OR A PILL OR A DRILL OR A SCALPEL?

WHAT A LOOK!

I DROOL TO GET MY FINGER-NAIL NEEDLES INTO YOUR PRETTY HEAD! SLICE THOSE FROWN MUSCLES! TIGHTEN UP THOSE ATROPHIED SMILE MUSCLES!

LISTEN, IS MY BROTHER CURED?

OH, NO! SOMEONE'S SWIPED HIS HEART AND SOUL! BABY CAN NO LONGER ROCK 'N' ROLL!

HE'LL WITHER AND DIE, DIE AND WITHER.

SECOND LAW OF THERMO-DYNAMICS-- ALL SYSTEMS BREAK DOWN-- TO DUST!

THAT'S HIS FATE-- A DUST HEAP!

UNLESS, YOU PREFER A MERCY KILLING?

COME HERE, YOU JUICY PIECE OF STEAK!

I PROMISE-- NO PAIN! YOU GOT THE BRAIN, I GOT THE SCALPEL!

YOU GOT THE BODY, I GOT THE COFFIN!

SHUT UP! YOU'VE GOT TO CURE HIM!

WHEN IN DOUBT, CUT! IT'S THE DOCTOR'S WAY!

Sney!

YOU'RE ALL SICK AND PATHETIC! I'M GOIN' HOME.

43

44

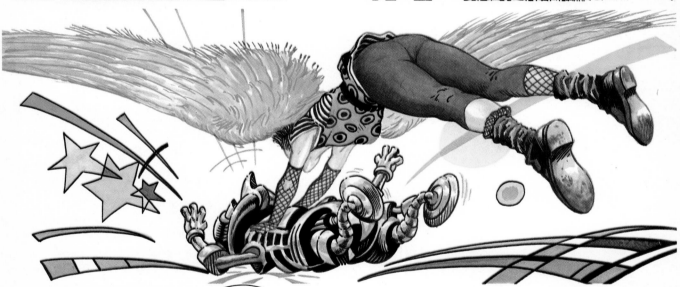

THANKS, JOY. YOU SAVED HIM.

WOW. YOU'VE ACTUALLY GOTTEN NICE!

AH... SHUT UP.

IT WAS FUN. IN FACT, NOW I'M PSYCHED TO KILL THAT BOGEY!

I NEED A HERO! I'M GONNA BUILD ONE!

STARS AN' STRIPES!

WINGED FEET! A CAPE!

ALL RIGHT! BIG MUSCLES! ARMS LIKE POPEYE!

A SQUARE JAW!

A BARREL CHEST!

SPIDER-MAN'S WEBS!

IRON MAN'S ROCKETS!

GOOD WORK, MEN!

Oh, NO! JUST MY LUCK!

BACK TO YOU TWO LITTLE TOADS AGAIN.

'ULLO?

GUESS I FELL *ASLEEP*...

COULD'A SWORN I *FELL*.

KNOW THAT FEELING, WHEN YOU'RE ABOUT TO FALL ASLEEP...

...AN' YOU'RE WOKEN UP WITH A START 'CAUSE YOU FEEL LIKE YOU FELL AN' HIT THE BED?

YEAH...

WHAT ABOUT IT?

WHAT THE HECK AM I EVEN *DOING* HERE WITH YOU TWO? I'M SPLITTIN'.

SHOULDN'T YOU LITTLE BRATS BE HOME IN BED?